"Internal time stretched and stilled,
inattentive to the minutes and hours
outside of itself."

–Zadie Smith, NW

PLACES
WHERE WE CAN IMAGINE
A BOOK OF LOVE POEMS

BY MAYA ODIM

This book is dedicated to the loved ones who
teach me by example to:
keep my Trap House clean, pay attention,
and practice love.

Published in 2014 by Udala Press
P.O. Box 6366 | Evanston, IL 60204

ISBN: 978-0-9846866-1-2
Printed in the United States of America

Graphic Design: Greta Carlson
The bodytext of the poetry is typeset in Chaparral Pro Light
9.5/11.5pt. Titles and details are typeset in Avenir.

10 9 8 7 6 5 4 3 2 1

CONTENTS

MOUNTAIN 11

CEREMONY 12

1, 4, 3 14

"YOUR SILENCE WILL NOT SAVE YOU."
– AUDRE LORDE 15

THE RISK 17

NIGHT ON US, DAY ON US 27

HAIKU 28

THE RUN 29

UNTITLED 35

PLACING EYES IN THERE 38

CYPHER 40

"LAND GONNA CHANGE HANDS" 42

HERE WE ARE 46

DEDICATION 47

HANGING THE MOON 49

EVERYTHING, SCATTER 51

NEW SOBER 55

RHAPSODY OR CHOPPED AND SCREWED 56

MOUNTAIN

To believe in your love I have to believe
    in my ability to love.

Wishing for this to be a certain way
    would make this something else,
now it is old and new in me.
It has to be what it is (even if my heart breaks).
I want it to be what it is now because even at times
    when I want *more* than this, I want *this*.

CEREMONY

The problem is I keep trying to catch you
    knowing I am not to be caught,
you are no promised land and neither am I.
Our bodies are continents and boats.
Promises are bodies of thought in flux,
they don't mean possession and they don't mean
    permanent, they are hooks on tongues that can
    be removed.

I think you think I need you to name us,
    but that is not my preoccupation.

I wonder, how do we acknowledge what it means
    to rely on each other?
Recognize and share it, let ourselves be in it...
    and if we haven't promised each other something
does that mean we've promised each other nothing?

Action is 9/10 of reality
there are promises to make but no truths
    assured by them,
possession is 9/10 of the law
there are promises to make but no bodies
    secured by them,
belief is 9/10 of hope
there are promises to make but no eternity
    procured by them.

I can only ceremony.

Our boats dock on the shore of a clearing
   (where we have built no house) we pattern our
   way to regularly.

1, 4, 3

Haiku

Orthopedic act,
healing springs our nature to
talk eternal talk.

"YOUR SILENCE WILL NOT SAVE YOU." – AUDRE LORDE

from "The Transformation of Silence into Language and Action"

It's necessary to talk.
Talk is so easily criticized but we need it, even if only
    as an exercise of memory.
I don't know how to talk about this, what if memory
    turns into museum?
We know what that can do to a people,
    and to people,
how it can get you to believe you have everything
    in front of you to understand what has come
    before you
and gets you believing the only truth is in what
    you're viewing
leaving you to wonder how what you see once
    existed and does no more?

But not if it's told true, no second guessing:
*Thewailingahollowsoundthatfloatedonthewindfromtwo-
blocksawaythewordsweremuffledbuttheagonywasclear-
notknowingwhatwashappeningbutknowingthatsome-
thingwashappeningatfirstitsoundedlikeawomanwas-
mourningthedeathofsomeoneasthewindcarriedhervoice-
andafterhearingtheshotsitbecameclearshewaswailing-
becausesheknewshewasgoingtodie.*

They were lovers. He killed her.

> rebel
> re, be
> l[ive]

I imagine someone listening might then say,
    "I don't mean this in a bogus way, but why
    are you telling me this."
And I'd reply, "because, we're in this together."

    the impossibility of changing reality?

Then for many reasons they might ask hopelessly/
    skeptically, "so how do we change reality?"
And I would simply reply with, "by being real."

THE RISK

It's time. The sun is melting orange and the moon is dropping shadows: hiding on top of/underneath/ on top of/underneath the clouds. Outside leaves are crinkling easily because bare bones are almost here, as we are rotating out of fall. There are sayings of death coming in threes, Lotti laughs to herself thinking: The mind, body and spirit! The Father, Son and Holy Ghost! Red, blue and yellow! Three strikes, you're out! Three strikes 'till lock-up! Rebel, rebel, rebel, rebel! And if no one is counting for her she is allowing herself as many chances as needed before proclaiming death, or another's death, or the death of what they have worked on together. Words play across her teeth xylophone like: *Let go*. A pot of lentils on the stove is reaching ready, usually over cooked tonight they don't over reach.

"Ready or not..." listening to an album Lotti decorates herself after food. Fresh and with a full stomach she gets on her bike. Mouthing a conversation to herself as she peddles, getting to where she's going gets her to the end of this day dream.

Lotti locks up her bike and walks down the block to the lounge. Reaching around the room, making eye contact as their hands say hello and hugging others who don't speak the dialect. She walks through a crowd of people to get to the cypher. Warming up the palms of her hands and the heels of her feet, trajectory has been plotted, she jumps in.

[mo]ving   AND $s^h{}_ak_in^g$

Lotti finishes her set and freezes. Walking out of the cypher a friend comes around asking for her company outside.

–What's up? You look tiiiired.
–I am, and I feel like giving up...on love. Lotti, is love bullshit?
–Nooooo, because imagination is not bullshit and if that's not the start of love, then what is?
–I can imagine all I want but that doesn't mean what I imagine will become a part of my reality.
–And that's exactly it! Love is about compromise and imagination is about possibility....cosmic sloppiness! The chance that love might grow.
They chuckle.
–Unified mess! If only. I don't know if my lover wants a unified anything, but I keep coming around 'cause he's so hospitable!
They both look at each other laughing and rapping:
"I really know how it feels to be stressed out, stressed out When you're face to face with your adversityyyy."
–Ha. I'm worried, I know this is going to hurt when it ends but it is not hurting now, so do I need to stop it? Preemptive strike? ...what does he think?

What am I thinking??? He's strong, doesn't show
any worry. Maybe if I act like him, like a "boy"
I can get through it unscathed.

Looking into her eyes Lotti can see it, her fear
won't help her, a preemptive strike won't save
her heart nor will withholding passion. How to
channel the energy, maybe into purposefulness?
Into confidence?

−But it sounds like you are hurting now. Gurl,
 everyone is capable of being hurt, even the boys.
 It's no competition, you do not need to be stronger
 than or as strong as anyone else...maybe time to
 peace out of this relationship?
−Ha! If only I knew *if* it was a relationship!
−Well don't y'all rely on each other for stuff?
−...maybe? I'm out, I have to be out because I don't
 have time for a relationship anyway.
−Ha! This balance is nothing new. All life is, is
 relationships, from them you cannot hide!
Shaking their heads chuckling. They look at each
other speaking at the same time,
−Let it go?!
They walk back inside, each believing they'd
stumbled upon some type of wisdom. A cypher
opens up again and Lotti jumps in.

Quick, indecisive. In her head as she breaks:
    We think that if he tells us he may hurt us

then he is the one.
Because he's honest.
We think that if we know what might
happen ain't nothing wrong with embarking
on that journey
fore we know where the road will lead,
we can pack accordingly?

> People try to make it seem like
> any rational
> present in this century mufucka,
> wouldn't believe in love, in any
> romantic sense.

> *Believe in lust and entrapment!*
> *Believe in regret!*
> *Trust but verify!*

> Call that loyalty?

Surprising isn't it?
How someone can release you and you can
feel caught
how sight can trigger feeling
how smell can taste sweet
how sleeping can awaken your mind's eye
how not holding back can protect your heart

ready?

How wandering can bring the clearest direc-
tion at times when the clock doesn't matter
how people, the number of them can be of
little importance compared to the quality of
the individuals in a group
how something comes from nothing
how learning can come from anything
how healing has to come from many things
we do with purpose
how pencil is as permanent as pen on paper
as tag on brick
as sand castle amongst a wind storm because
of memory
   remember: this too shall pass!

   Love is real because imagination is
   real, and if that's not the beginning of
   love sometimes, then what is?

Lotti freezes.

The lot of them rock out. As the night becomes
confident they hear,
–Last call! Hanging on until they can no longer,
outside and chilling until. They become wandering
bodies because what they have at that moment is
each other and whatever they think of, all thinking
differently. There for the duration, then until comes
and Lotti heads home. In the wind. On the bike. By
the time she gets there the night is on balance beam.

Fast asleep she falls quick into bed, and dreams:

> Looking at her he says: Your back, it looks
> strong. I can't figure it out because I see
> you're hollow.
> She replies: Figure what out? I leave space,
> you need space to store stuff.
> –You plan for storage? Never thought of that.
> –I know we just met, but I gotta say, you
> smell nice.
> –Thanks. You're beautiful.
> She smiles.
> –I read somewhere Jimi Hendrix once said:
> I don't like compliments because they're
> distracting.
> He smiles.
> –It wasn't a compliment.
> A few fish are swimming around the wooden
> floor they're standing on, in between their
> feet in a figure-eight, patterning. He looks
> down, and looks up at her:
> –You ever been fishing?
> –Only a couple times.
> –I know this place around the way that'll lend
> us some rods and hooks…
> –How do we get there?
> –Running. Through this forest,
> –Running! I like how you think!
> –I'm always ready for a footrace!
> –I'll race with you but I don't think I'm fast

enough to race anyone to get to you.
–What are you thinking about? There is no
one here but us.

The forest they are running through is wide.
Leaf covered hills, trees and just as many
twigs. Upon reaching a clearing in front of
the water they stop and stand still. Imitating
its edge, warming up their palms and the
heels of their feet. Then sitting shoulder to
shoulder they wait. Revealed. Fishing. Piling
Lake Trout on either side of themselves.
Greens that looked like greens and blues
that looked like blues on each fish. Turning
around they find fire. Taking turns they add
fish. Not throwing away a thing, using bones
to make necklaces and tooth pics, sewing
needles and sculptures. Looking up they see
the North Star. Everything browns evenly.

He laments, I don't have any black pepper. I'll
remember next time.
She assures, no matter, the meal is good as is.
I didn't come expecting anything other than
the food we'd catch. And the run.
And I probably won't be back so, don't worry
about remembering pepper.
Jolted he wonders, Why? Why won't you be
back? How do you know?
–I know. Because it will take too long for me

to find you and I will give up looking.
–I'll send a signal. You can sniff me out
remember!
–Sniff you out, with your pockets full of black
pepper!
–I'm bringing it for us. And I'm supposed to
find you when your shape changes because
you add to storage! You ask me questions
you need to be asking yourself.
–I didn't even ask you anything.
–Oh you didn't?
–You'll forget. Everything.
–I'm not looking to forget, I remember you
right now.
–Me? Under what circumstances, there is no
one else here. Of course you remember me.
–The fish are here!
–Fish don't count!
–Ms. Earth sign, and now fish don't count?
Everything has a spirit. Well I'm here, and
I'm not thinking about myself I'm thinking
about you.
–Are you looking for me?
–I thought I'd found you here.
–I knew you'd forget...
–Forget what?
Lotti:
Him:

They picked at the rest of the fish bones for any remaining meat and leaned their backs against a tree to rest.

–I don't think I got your name.
–It's Lotti. What's yours?
–...that's what they call me.

Looking behind the tree they're leaning against Lotti finds some watermelon sliced, they split it. The sounds of a copper spit bucket ring out as seeds land in front of them.

–Over there!
–Over there!
–Right there!
–Right there!

Talking less and less, playing more and more, Lotti feels the need to reposition herself and leans her back against another part of the same tree. The weight of the shift causes this piece to snap in half. Her back hits the ground, bruising. The piece she was leaning against snapped in half because it was a twig, disguised by the tree it was near.

He blurts out: On second thought, let's not make plans to come back together. You come

back if you want to, but you don't have to
wait for me to do so.
–I thought we'd decided you'd send a signal?
And what if I want to wait?
–You can if you want to...I guess.
–You're thinking, *why would I.*
–You don't know what I'm thinking.
–I'm ready for a journey, a foot race, remem-
ber? Each other?
–No. I'm saying don't wait for me, just run.
–
–

Lotti lets out: But I'm strong enough.
He asks her to take it back: That doesn't
matter right now.
–
–

–Got it.

The next day Lotti wakes up late, with mourning
already in her bed.

NIGHT ON US, DAY ON US

Two fires burning
flames jumping
two wells
filling buckets
many minds
thoughts tangling
two bodies
tumbling
a W and an E.

Enterrados.

Reconstituted clay.
Our rocks have been sifted out,
our sticks have been set aside
our water drained through cloth
falling, landing on dirt
sinking through layers of earth
mixing into ground water
filling wells we fill buckets from.

The planets welcome our orbits
night on us
day on us
clouds decorating
cement suffocating.
Worrying
Exhaling

HAIKU

Transparency = tool.
Dig this as strategy. Earth
has no cards, is real.

THE RUN

Tomorrow is already happening yet the sky is still
a deep purple from the night before. Some yellows
from the sun rising in, mixing with moon's shadows.
Dorothy, the butcher down the block, raises pigs
in an abandoned lot behind her house. Sometimes
looking out into the front yard Lotti can feel some-
one standing behind her when she's thinking of the
pigs. Her grandmother told her that the women in
their family reincarnate as birds but she gathers that
someone must be in that pig. Remembering she has
to water the flowers:

> water as a place to gather around
> water as conduit to the spirits
> water as conduit to birth and rebirth
> transculturation
> (her back)
> as forgetting, as getting free, as springing
> from, as running over

Purple runs away from the sky as she gives water
location in the garden out front, she and her
neighbor share land so they can have more room for
planting. Lotti is always imagining. Like when she is
watering, she practices coming home (the packing/
the carrying, the arriving, most exciting is the
leaving), pretending she is going somewhere when

she goes to get the hose and coming home after watering as if she's ever left her yard. Sometimes pretending she is meeting him, the only time they truly share place is when she's imagining. Always writing or thinking so they can make together through the conjuring of her words. The place of her forevers. There are times when she only wants him in thought, in no practical or physical form at all.

Once she dreamt he forgot he knew her:

> Through the windows of the train you can see the sun cut across the water like mango knife cutting blueberries. Lotti thinks, *how have I peeled apart in front of him I am not a mango?*
> She lives tiptoeing. Sensing some shift she feels before thinking and spits out: You and me still, right?
> He answers: I'm not sure if I remember what you and me is.
> –You said it one time, we decided, a W and an E. Don't you remember the fire?
> –I remember fire, but not a fire we made.
> –Maybe I'm mistaken, but you smell just like a fire I started to cook dinner last night.
> –I know them, fires. But I don't ever make them. Are you sure you're not misremembering?
> –Nosotros anoche, olvidaste.

–I'm sorry I don't speak Spanish.
–Olvidaste.

The train is moving in directions no one is
plotting because their mission is to leave
where they've come from and get where
they are going. They'll know once they arrive.
When coming home they will keep track of
direction. Lotti has no spell for memory loss
so she decides to leave the cabin, maybe she
can find someplace to leave her memories.
Roaming the train Lotti finds a place she
can rest. Just as large but different from the
dining car and the lounge car this one is
filled with four daybeds covered in Zebra
skin. She's been told they'll help you tumble,
and imagines: *And you want to tumble.*
Taking her time lying down on each of them
she follows some pattern. Around the space
there are maps on the walls, drawings of
what she reads as galaxies and what she can
only imagine to be travel patterns. Looking
up, plants going through osmosis. You could
imagine you were alone, but what's the
point? People were always there.

She doesn't know how but the tumbling
moved her back to her cabin, arriving Lotti
finds her love asleep there. Lying back down
she prepares to journey with him.

The snapping of twigs on the ground brings Lotti into the hand of her found again lover. They travel back across the forest to another clearing, happening upon a field of blackberries. Turning around bushes are now lining their perimeter. Walking and talking and picking berries they rekindle.

–I didn't bring a bag to carry these in.
–We'll just eat our take.
–Did I ever tell you about my parents' house?
–Not yet.
–My parent's had this room in the basement called the study.
–Did you ever go in?
–Always.

Twisting cheeks and lips because a sour berry made it on the tongue.

–When I was a kid, I would imagine being an adult in there. Now I'm growing and it's nothing like I imagined.
–Go on.
–Feels like I'm always fighting against not being consumed by something. A lover, a bunch of haters, the promise of land. Guilt.
–That's being human.
–Sometimes I feel like I'm fighting against being engulfed by Humanness. Aren't we

animal too? I need less control, less predictability. I need more preparation, more practice. More faith

A twinge in her stomach makes Lotti's mouth shut, drawing her hand to her belly, she's eaten too many blackberries. Her mind distracted she can only think of looking for water. They roam.

Lotti wakes up to the train slowing down, she is in the cabin alone now. Maybe because her love went to the daybeds? The drink cart passes by warming the air with coffee. Getting up and sitting down Lotti drinks from her cup. Waiting. Thinking if she thinks hard enough they'll come back, she hopes.

The train approaching higher and higher speeds Lotti realizes that slow down was actually a speed up, the beginning of a gradual climb. Catching her off guard she panics and it comes out. The screams, she lets it out. Reaching for the window for the back of her lover's head: I just want to see the back of your head! Why have you left me without letting me see you leave!? How can I let go without seeing you leave? I can handle goodbye but I can't handle being left!! Where are you going??

–I'm going mad.

Some time later the train reaches its final
platform. Doing nothing but trying to
prepare for the rest of her journey Lotti is
hungry, she needs meat. Seasoned muscle.
Something to chew, release tension in her
jaw. A spirit to libate for providing her with
nutrition. She will give back to every lover
after. She will stop eating potatoes and bread
until she is healed. She is hungry, will only
eat meat. She will only eat pork, she will
ask any spirits present at the table to guide
her digestion. Of this, of her food. The
North star is bright in the sky, and her
breath makes trails in the air. Quite a change
from back home. Sneezing Lotti reaches
for a napkin, blowing her nose out comes
purple snot.

She folds it up, slips it in her pocket and
finds the exit.

UNTITLED,

for my brothers Chaka Patterson and Rashid Johnson

We change
We change because of this
as we think we can change others
as we misremember our histories
as we are learning to read
as death's meaning is changing
as we internalize
as we still favor marriage as a legal pretense
    for the sharing of assets and a social pretense
    for commitment,
as we support the canons we say we are troubling
    with equality
we are changing
because of this
because,
because of shell casings
because of memory
because we need each other
because birth happens
changing this
this need to close and reopen, to night and day.
    To, tomorrow.
This loss of ritual
these identities that lineage wealth
this language as cultural and capital
changing this

wading through this
rebirth because of this
conjuring because of this
absolutely
salt
tell
this
living this
performing this
and performing contradictions
By this, gifted wool.
By this, depleted.
by searching for permanence, forgetting about
    transition
made human because we make inhuman,
made the namer of all
we make what makes up history.
These pheromones are muted
losing scents, gaining brains and white teeth
we change because of these contradictions.
Born with no answers
born with no sin
born and caught,
made to promise
taught how to say some things before we know what
    they mean
taught to mean what we say
taught to keep our heads in the game
as education is so expensive
we change because of necessity

and try not to argue over experience
understand multiple languages
hook our tongues to promises
we are asked to maintain this by oaths and
    allegiance
not hidden at all
          how do we change reality?
by being real
you don't have to know the pain to feel the hurt
    sometimes
you don't have to know the dance steps to enjoy
    the movement.
You can find the rhythm
Sifting, rearranging, fashioning new tools
whose *master*? whose narrative? whose house?
truth exists, rising no matter what legacy
    we think we leave
libate
be well
do you want to be healed?
how do you need to be healed?
Conjuring?
Dissolving?
we are born into this but not born to live this
we are arriving and creating
making next chapters

PLACING EYES IN THERE

I am big enough to fill you and you to overflow with
    the comfort of pushed edges
tangling smoothly beneath royal palms

Tall enough
broad
heavy footed
smiling enough

Fingers outstretched in air swooping down like

You captivate my hip movements
flying through, cupping air
sparks flying
my brains and their waves
and tiptoeing on sometimes jagged rocks
and melting into comfortably warm water
and jumping
and seeing new

You fly my arms up and around
you ache my heels
stretch me wide
drench me in salt waters.

Drenching us in salt waters
bouncing us wildly north.

Stretching my memory
right along side my arms
right along side my lower calf
comfortably pushing my edges
howling through my back/my back/my back
and placing eyes in there
you crack my hips pivoting me boundless

CYPHER

A cypher is a compost heap
receives nutrition
circular
radiates heat like compost
is filled with stacks of everything that has
    been released
the anticipation, the energy, the ease,
if they breed as such birth children, and children's
    children.

A cypher is living like a human being,
looks different each time like a human being

Can be lost challenging courage,
sometimes needs to be opened up.
Some times has a crack in the bottom and loses its
    middle (falling through the hole in the bucket
    dear Liza, the hole)

A cypher is what it can maintain as galaxy.
It is defined by its space,
what people we call artists would call:
    its negative space.
Defined by what it can be taken up with.

As its elements break us down:
cypher leaves trails of happenings,

makes eye contact
eyeballs and third eye
welcomes lungs to fill
welcomes muscles to tear
welcomes getting it right
welcomes losing your way
no pre-form
no conform
a cypher is organic like people have been living for
    centuries.
Living off of the land.
A cypher is nothing new.
Cypher trades and barters for what's in season

Cypher is family like family inherits
cypher moves with us,
centuries, timeless, cockroach skeleton, cosmic slop
    lineage
a cypher has been around the block
a cypher is family like family inheritance that
    trumps blood
cypher is spade
cypher eat
cypher breath
under the bed at night cypher ghost!
See you/see me,
cypher hide and go seek!

Through the view find or are we found?
Cypher be.

"LAND GONNA CHANGE HANDS"

HANDS: I have this friend who worries she lets it out too often.

LAND: A friend? *Well*, tell your *friend* worrying it was let out too often is futile because that probably only happens once it's been released. Let it out when it can be held in no longer because something is bubbling up saying, "es el tiempo!" There is a fine balance between what we need and what will benefit others, try and find that balance.

HANDS: You really think she should let it out? I've noticed it turns some people away. They say (they act like) it *looks* and *smells* too bad and it's too *noisy*.

LAND: It turns some people away? Why does it matter who it turns away? Do these people stop and talk? Want to have a conversation, recognize her as like them enough to have a reason for her doings? If they don't have the time to do that, then why does she think they'd have time to notice if she's letting it out or not?

You have to let it out, it's the byproduct of
a reaction. It's matter and prefers to move
from a place that's crowded to a place that
can be filled.

HANDS: How do you know this? Where
does it come from then?

LAND: I know this because I've practiced it. It
comes from within blood, but not the way
these people say, *oh, they have it in their blood.*
This thing you're letting out, it conjures
from within.
Has a spirit you can feel.
A spirit you can learn. These people you talk
about, that judge her, they can learn it too.

HANDS: How?

LAND: It's about what's happening. It's about
not hiding anything from your spirit and
understanding that if you do it starts to ruin
you. Starts to rot you from within. Starts to
ferment your blood, and not in the healthy
way like from juice to wine or vinegar, the
unhealthy way like gangrene. I'm guessing
she figured this out, so she let's it out, all of
that spirit and those Santas and growth and
new growth all of that being.

It's about recognizing that we are not here
alone, not in this alone, not creating this
alone, not dealing with this alone, not
accepting this alone, not fixing this alone,
not loving this alone, not living this alone,
not the only ones forgetting this, not the
only ones remembering this.

HANDS: Believing?

LAND: Think about it like this: put in work.

HANDS: I do work.

LAND: Girly girl, you have not yet learned how
to work with naturally occurring elements
you only know how to work with elements
you've created. The latter is a good practice
but not the only thing to practice. Work with
the former and you'll see, everything takes
on new meanings, different than you've
been conditioned to think them to mean.
Outside, inside, on-top of, change too. Your
sinew, and fat and muscle change shape also.
Your body learns to cradle, the heels of your
hands learn to contain, the palms of your
hands learn to usher. Your fingers pinch
and gather, list and rearrange, have neces-
sary reflex. This is told to your body. This, is
rhythm.

It's about rhythm.

If told to your body, then you are knowledge-
able in the universal sense of the word.
The contrapositive: If you have no rhythm
it's because knowledge has not been shared
with your body.

The long and short of it, what's necessary
for some parts of your life is not sufficient
for all parts. No matter what you know, you
have to know how to dance because rhythm
is knowledge manifest.

HANDS:

HERE WE ARE

We know how to pack
together we gather, think that ordering our
    chaos will bring us closer to understanding
    our memories.
Sometimes we talk so long the day feels short;
finding ourselves watching the night as it's on
    balance beam
back bending to catch the sun's attention,
a gaggle of us.
Trying hard to remember the direction in what can
    feel like misdirected emotion.
Relying on everything even when we say we,
    "only rely on certain things."
Here we are.

DEDICATION

Woman comes heavy,
fleshed out
weighted
thick, stuck together and overflowing
near, imperfect, creative, perceptive, receptive
    and clear.

                        Wandering
and ready.

Women know how to run
hang out in air that holds truth as a scent
sometimes sit circular like they are working on
    something (we are famous for second chances)
they are working on something,
working on woman.
Telling the stories of how this means more than
    dresses or no dresses
means more than having hair long, or more
    "importantly" straight.
means more than tracking your cycle by the moon,
means more than the cycle only a moon can bring
    (then believing, and then not believing in magic)
means more than always having an ultimatum,
    hearing others warn,
–You know, you don't get free like that.
    –You *know* you don't get free like that.

–You know you don't get free like that.
–Sabes que?
I'm not trying to be free, already been there.
I'm trying to be me, and I am woman.

When I say woman I mean I am wild.
"Wild women don't wear no blues"
 memorize no half composed tunes
 or forget how to groove.
"Wild women don't wear no blues."
 Do build with reusable tools
 recycle like it's nothing new
 remember where their hips come from
 mujeres antepasadas y el mar tan azul
"wild women don't wear no blues."
Can't always figure them out...
wild women
brick house
bonita
mamajama
sweet honey b-gurl
wild women are life, say life
bring with them decorations of all types and
seasons
<u>wild women need a rhyme and a reason</u>
              wild women are nothing new,
                    "wild women don't wear no blues"

HANGING THE MOON

Between us there are goats,
bellies full.
strawberry. We making sense enough to babble
brooks line pathways to trading grounds
bartering our way to stableness.
Exchanging energy,
so cup your arms,
bend this branch here so we know from
    whence we came,
always there
always a beacon
timeless with yes. Finishing for tomorrow
sagging in the direction the moon hangs.

Hanging the moon
sure footed
round
sweet and making sense enough to babble
brooks line pathways to trading grounds
bartering our ways to stableness,
exchanges of energy and,
filling lungs. So cup your arms,
bend this branch backwards so you know from
    where we came
always there
always here, a beacon
timeless as we measure.

Sagging in the direction the moon hangs between us
goats,
timeless in our measure of distance
ere we reach fertile ground,
planting soil...
I used to think you hung the moon
I will remember thinking that
and revel in the joy.

Your belly is full of goats
seasoned and roasting over hot coals

EVERYTHING,
SCATTER

You, me, water, ocean, Middle Passage, just...yes.
Metaphor, between the sheets, patience, love,
lingering, lemons. Margarita w/ sugar instead of
salt. Spice, everything in between. Nervous, juice,
potatoes, garlic. No Bread. Oven kitchen, my
parent's kitchen. My grandmother polishing brass
cabinet handles, photography, Gumbo, travel,
conversations, first dates, forests
you, me, goats.

Don't be afraid unless you are invited, then don't
anticipate. Don't expect, let patience be your armor.
Warrior, alone, desperation, camp, tents, moonlight,
army: bullshit:: love: savior, us, savory. Ear drum,
Jazz hum.
Learn about patience then throw yourself over your
backside. Reach. A friend one time, looking exactly
like themselves said, they are, "a force to be beck-
oned with."

Language is developed.

Strike while the iron is hot. Reconcile
yourself to the possibility of next lifetimes.

You've found each other when you know you want to

decompose together.
Let go of whatever you feel you need to with no
regrets.
You will be okay because we love you.
I can not protect you but life can.

Calling you with a loving call, with ease like steam
rising from something hot. With case. Still I hurt,
with a pain that is so far from surface it turns my
insides right way around.
Roaming.

>We're not going back to each other.

The skin is not a scar. The way it moves once it's
gained presence and topples over itself relaxing
into space
we are these stackings of cosmic slop and through
the view find, or are we found? It must be
tough to be here representing our selves. Looking
for meaning in the ways our hips rock and what
we perceive as our insides accomplish. That heart.
That brain. That spirit? The body has circles bends
itself backwards over others. Everything but
spillage because skin encases and represents these
meanings we know nothing of.

We fumble in the dark for whom? Them? They need
us not.

These meanings from our skins how? Can we take color to mean spirit and joy, because we have meant deliverance. If we take color to mean anything, can it be, at most spectrum? After we've built it to mean ownership, spirit, love, drums, head, movement, reliability, knowledge, worth, crumb cake, cherries, meat loaf, plantains, cereal, lemons, dirt.

So our hearts are in our chests now?

Facing forward, the world is a circle and who has the means to view it through space travel, who told us this of its shape? And without a comfortable place to sleep for the many, can we be powder puff and ask, who has a place to explore uninterrupted dreams? Can we be warrior like and ask, who has a space to explore uninterrupted dreams?

Docent, chains, museums, chocolate, pecans, sweat.

You, me, relationships, English is your second language. Distance. People look at us weird even when we are ourselves.
So who are we left to be if we are thinking of raising children and decomposing?

> Ourselves no matter what. Whatever we
> raise, whatever we fertilize needs us to be
> ourselves.

We need wealth for generations in more than
cash flow, though disposable income makes living
clothing, transportation, meals, getting to school,
getting home from school, visiting ancestral
lands, grooming, having a place to rest one's body
for periods of uninterrupted dreaming less about
surviving. Can't we change that? We need beckon-
ings. English is your second language, I am your
third. We need to learn more.

And you look at me like you're thinking, I'm trying
to learn how to love you. I'm thinking, I want to
learn to love you, and let go of everyone's expecta-
tions so there is energy left to provide these bodies
we may raise with weather, potatoes, climbing, paint,
muscles, eyes, tongues, finding security in distinct
nomadic hearts and livers.

On paper someone tells us both to smolder our
experience to think: you are this, I am that. You are
there, I am here. But I feel you here as
I am this.

NEW SOBER

Coming to you like water comes to rain,
    trailing behind itself.
Wandering and ready.
The only thing I'm sure of is that withholding
    passion won't heal me.

I am not living a poem.

I am not a mango. How is it I've peeled apart in
    front of you?
I can no longer serve you my heart because
    I've run out of ways to cook it.

RHAPSODY
OR
CHOPPED AND SCREWED

there
be
here
here
when
I
think
of
you,
even
when
you're
not
near.
Oceans
don't
separate
they
make
bigger
the
space
we
have
to

like
(love)
each
other
in,
learn
to.
This
world
be
bigger
with
oceans
full
like
a
gourd
for
us
to
pour
from...
u
be
wind
I
be
viento.
One
and

the
same.
Two
paths
arriving
where
we
arrive
or traveling to where we wish to be...

    -eef our gawd e's gawd

    ...you ah prain eentoo da fewcha
    ...you ah prain eentoo our fewcha
    ...you ah prain eentoo yah chewdrens fewcha
    repen!
    repen!
    repen!
    repen!
    repen!
    yeeeeeeeeeeeehhhhh!

    ...eef you pray eentoo da fewcha you pray!
    ...eef you pray eentoo da fewcha you pray!

If our god is God there is no promised land.
Remember you're not afraid of the dark,
you're afraid of what you think is in
The Dark:

Boogie Man, Monsters in the closet,
Monsters under the bed, Monsters live in
the Dark because Dark should be feared

Color:	Black
Eating:	Devil's Food Cake
Shunned:	Black Listed, Tar Baby, Black Sheep in the Family, Nigger
Catastrophe:	Black Friday, Burnt, why is it so dark?
Shadows:	Black Out, Black Hole
Driving:	Black Ice
Market:	Black Friday

They all took

Advice:	los vicios que se adornan la mente son más difícil soltar que los en la mano.
Advice:	you give too much of yourself in the beginning. I don't mean sex, I mean of your heart.

They all took some shit they ain't never give back.
Make me want forever/sober.

I don't want to tell people about you/I want
to tell everyone about us
I worry that bringing what is here into the
realm of what is there will not add to our
happiness.

And I have reduced us to happiness and I
have reduced myself to a worrying woman.
We are ever changing and I believe that
my love for you will never change? We are
individuals and I have reconciled myself to
the idea of an us?

> HANDS: 'Cause maybe we are reaching for
> the wrong people?

LAND: Don't say wrong.

> HANDS: Ok. Maybe we are misunderstand-
> ing the people we reach for.

LAND: It's one of three things:
1) he isn't attracted to female identified bodies
2) he is attracted to female identified
bodies, he doesn't like you
3) his heart is somewhere else.
Don't settle. I don't even know what to
tell you anymore, you don't have to turn
your life upside down when things aren't
working out.

> HANDS:

LAND: Acknowledge.

> HANDS: He's not the one I'm looking for.

60

LAND: Think. You walk away from every love.
Even the dudes who dump you, you dump
yourself. You're always leaving something.

HANDS: Because I'm looking for things
in-between what they give me,
seeing colors I've imagined to be
there because I hear that this here
is to bring colors.
Looking for patience to fashion
into armor...
There is a softness that writes
itself in-between the creases of
his lips
a longing his hands give me
a need to make present attention
to the way I breathe,
make sure the breaths are deep
enough
cause this is the point when the
core has a chance to awaken
in order to connect...

LAND: To connect with what?
You will know when you're ready to commit
to someone, even though it means not being
with others.

HANDS: I believe he is someone.

LAND: You can not be prevented.
    I am talking about self discovery
    I am talking about being well.

    How do you take care of something so that it
    consistently yields?
    Yourself?
    Love?
    Your garden?

    By nourishing what's in season.
    By being the natural woman or human you are.

    Health is complex.

    I mean our spirits when I talk about health.

HANDS: Is it unhealthy to miss all the time?
    Or to be frustrated with memory?
    One time he said to me: it's hard to
    let a pretty girl go
    (and I almost let that trick me)
    One time he called me: nurse
    (and I almost forgot.)
    One time he called me: brown
    sugar (and I miss it)

LAND: *he* called *you?* ...remember what you call
    yourself.

HANDS: Wandering and ready.
Wild.
Woman.
Precise and purposeful!

In the affirmative.
I do not miss him all the time
only the times when I forget it
didn't work. Us lives in a place of
imagination, when we are together
there I'm sad for my reality here.
But without this real sadness my
imagination would not have its
happiness, for now at least. But
this too shall pass.

LAND: Yes!

Don't run from your pain, and don't hide
it with clutter. It goes in no hole, goes
underneath no rug. It needs to be eaten,
then shat out, then used as fertilizer.

There will be someone as long as you risk
and run and risk and run and plan and
notice and find and breathe and fill and
release and make time for your being.
Girly girl make time for your being. We
can not protect you, but life can.

Do you want me to tell you something really
    subversive?
Love is everything it's cracked up to be.
That's why people are so cynical about it.
It really is worth fighting for, being brave for,
risking everything for.
And the trouble is,
if you don't risk anything, you risk even more.

                    -Erica Jong

NOTES

"THE RISK"
"Ready or not..." Lyrics from the Fugees song, *"Ready Or Not"*.

"I really know how it feels to be stressed out, stressed out. When you're face to face with your adversity." Lyrics from the Tribe Called Quest song featuring Faith Evans, *"Stressed Out"*.

"THE RUN"
The train car where Lotti finds the day beds and the plants and the patterns on the walls was inspired by a work by my brother, Rashid Johnson, titled, *Shelter*.

"UNTITLED"
This was written in response to a Charles Bukowski poem, *Dinosauria We*.

The lines asking, "Whose master? Whose narrative? Whose house?" Are references to an essay by Audre Lorde titled "The Master's Tools Will Never Dismantle the Master's House", Sister Outside: essays and speeches (Crossing Press, Freedom, CA, 1984) and a speech by Manning Marable, given at Wesleyan University, 2007, where he talked about what he called, "the master narrative", or the narrative that's most often used to tell a certain history or story.

"CYPHER"

A cypher is another name for a circle. People have been gathering in cyphers for centuries, to talk or tell story, to sing and dance. It is used many times in this book to reference the circle created by Break Dancers. A cypher can be a stage or a rehearsal space. It can facilitate conversation or be used as a platform for competition. A cypher is holy in all senses of the word.

"LAND GONNA CHANGE HANDS"

This title is a chant that was spoken during the Civil Rights Movement of the 1960s, in the United States.

"What time is it?"
"Nation time!"
"What's gonna happen?"
"Land gonna change hands!"

In this poem Land is working to change Hand's mind, giving new meaning to the phrase, 'land gonna change hands'.

"DEDICATION"

This piece and it's last line were inspired by a book edited by Marita Golden titled: Wild Women Don't Wear No Blues: Black Women Writers on Love, Men, and Sex, (Knopf Doubleday Publishing Group, New York, 1994).

ABOUT THE AUTHOR

MAYA EMMA NNENA
RUTH ODIM

is a daughter, younger sister, niece, granddaughter,
aunt, cousin and friend. She works as a teaching
artist and agrarian. Through farming in the city
and Ceramics, Spoken Word/Poetry, and dance she
builds with youth and adults, both leading and
co-leading workshops in and outside of Chicago.
Holding a BA in American Studies from Wesleyan
University '10, Middletown, Connecticut, Maya
lives in Chicago, traveling often.

www.ingramcontent.com/pod-product-compliance
Lightning Source LLC
Chambersburg PA
CBHW060425050426
42449CB00009B/2131

Milk

for

Little Ones

Recovering *our* Confessional Heritage #5

Recovering *our* Confessional Heritage

James M. Renihan, Editor-in-Chief
Richard C. Barcellos, Managing Editor

James M. Renihan, *Associational Churchmanship: Second London Confession of Faith 26.12-15*

Richard C. Barcellos, *The Covenant of Works: Its Confessional and Scriptural Basis*

James M. Renihan, *A Toolkit for Confessions: Symbolics 101—Helps for the Study of English Puritan Confessions of Faith*

Ryan C. Hodson, *Milk for Little Ones: An Introduction to the Baptist Catechism*